# What Lily Gets from Bee
## And Other Pollination Facts

**by Ellen Lawrence**

Consultants:

**Suzy Gazlay, MA**
Recipient, Presidential Award for Excellence in Science Teaching

**Dr. Robin Wall Kimmerer**
Professor of Environmental and Forest Biology
SUNY College of Environmental Science and Forestry, Syracuse, New York

**Kimberly Brenneman, PhD**
National Institute for Early Education Research, Rutgers University
New Brunswick, New Jersey

**BEARPORT**
PUBLISHING

New York, New York

**Credits**

Cover, © JulietPhotography/Shutterstock and © irin-k/Shutterstock; 3TL, © irin-k/Shutterstock; 3BL, © Quang Ho/Shutterstock; 3BR, © motorolka/Shutterstock; 4BL, © Kisialiou Yury/Shutterstock; 4R, © David Maska/Shutterstock; 5L, © irin-k/Shutterstock; 5R, © Tudor Catalin Gheorghe/Shutterstock; 6, © Kellis/Shutterstock; 7, © Corinne Lamontagne; 9, © Brian A. Jackson/Shutterstock and © James H. Robinson/Science Photo Library; 11, © Sue Laakso; 12, © happytan/Shutterstock; 13L, © Scott Prokop/Shutterstock; 13R, © 1stclassphoto/Shutterstock; 14, © kanusommer/Shutterstock; 14–15, © Jeff Schultes/Shutterstock; 16B, © abxyz/Shutterstock; 16–17, © Steve Byland/Shutterstock; 18, © Robin Bush/Getty Images; 19, © Chien Lee/FLPA; 20–21B, © Natalia D/Shutterstock; 21BL, © Scott Prokop/Shutterstock; 21CL, © 1stclassphoto/Shutterstock; 21T, © Kisialiou Yury/Shutterstock; 21CR, © Sue Laakso; 21BR, © Brian A. Jackson/Shutterstock and © James H. Robinson/Science Photo Library; 22C, © VladisChern/Shutterstock; 22B, © Wikipedia Creative Commons; 22R, © Ruby Tuesday Books Ltd; 23TL, © Julietphotography/Shutterstock; 23TC, © S & D & K Maslowski/FLPA; 23TR, © Sue Laakso; 23BL, © Brian A. Jackson/Shutterstock and © James H. Robinson/Science Photo Library; 23BC, © kanusommer/Shutterstock; 23BR, © kukuruxa/Shutterstock.

Publisher: Kenn Goin
Editorial Director: Adam Siegel
Creative Director: Spencer Brinker
Design: Elaine Wilkinson
Photo Researcher: Ruby Tuesday Books Ltd

*Library of Congress Cataloging-in-Publication Data*

Lawrence, Ellen, 1967–
    What lily gets from bee : and other pollination facts / by Ellen Lawrence.
        p. cm. — (Plant-ology)
    Includes bibliographical references and index.
    ISBN 978-1-61772-587-6 (library binding) — ISBN 1-61772-587-0 (library binding)
    I. Title.
    QK926.L39 2013
    576.8'75—dc23

                                   2012009602

For more information, write to Bearport Publishing Company, Inc., 45 West 21st Street, Suite 3B, New York, New York 10010. Printed in the United States of America.

10 9 8 7 6 5 4 3 2 1

# Contents

# An Important Visitor

It is a sunny, summer morning.

Pink, yellow, and orange lily flowers are growing in a garden.

Summer is the time of year when lilies make seeds—but they need help.

Luckily, a small helper arrives.

A honeybee lands on one of the lily flowers and crawls inside.

lilies growing in a garden

Why do you think the honeybee
is visiting the lily flower?

honeybee

A seed is
the part of a
flower that can grow
into a new plant. Each
flower on a lily plant
makes hundreds
of seeds.

lily flower

5

# A Sweet Treat for Honeybee

anthers

Inside the lily, the bee drinks nectar.

It is a sweet liquid that flowers make.

Lilies also make a colored dust called **pollen**.

Pollen comes from a part of the flower called the **anthers**.

As the bee looks for nectar inside the flower, some pollen sticks to its furry body.

> What do you think the honeybee will do when it has finished drinking nectar from the lily flower?

6

pollen

anther

Honeybees carry some of the nectar they drink back to their **hive**. There, they turn the nectar into honey. They eat the honey in winter when there are no flowers around.

# Pollen on the Move

When the bee has finished drinking, it flies to a different flower and crawls inside.

Pollen is still stuck to its body.

As the bee looks for more nectar, some pollen brushes off its body.

It sticks to a part of the lily called the **stigma**.

The little bee doesn't know it, but it has just helped the lily make seeds!

A honeybee may be inside a flower for only a few seconds. Try to guess how many flowers a honeybee might visit in one day. (*Turn the page to find the answer.*)

8

stigma

pollen stuck to a honeybee

anther

Many flowers get honeybees to visit them by giving off a sweet smell. The smell is a sign to the bees that there is nectar inside the flowers.

# Honeybees Help Flowers

Spreading pollen from the anthers of one flower to the stigma of another is called **pollination**.

Honeybees are great **pollinators**.

When they visit a flower to drink nectar, pollen sticks to their bodies.

Then they spread the pollen as they fly from flower to flower to get more nectar.

A honeybee may visit about 2,000 different flowers in one day!

Draw a picture of a lily flower on a piece of paper. Then add these labels to your drawing:

- anther • pollen • stigma

You can look back through this book to make sure you put the labels in the correct places.

an anther
with pollen

pollen stuck
to a honeybee

Honeybees
carry some pollen
back to their hives.
There, the bees make
it into a food for
feeding baby
bees.

# Making Seeds

Inside the lily, some of the pollen left behind by the bee begins the process of making seeds.

The seeds grow inside a case that protects them.

The case is called a seedpod.

By fall, the seeds are fully grown.

The lily flower dies, and the seedpod splits open.

The seeds fall to the ground, ready to grow into new lily plants in the spring.

seedpod

seeds

Most flowers
need pollen from
another flower to make
seeds. Some flowers, such
as dandelions and those on
tomato plants, can use their
own pollen to pollinate
themselves.

lily seedpod

a new lily plant

# Insect Pollinators

Bees do more than just help lilies make seeds.

They also pollinate apple blossoms, roses, daisies, and many other types of flowers.

Bees aren't the only kind of insect that can pollinate flowers, however.

Butterflies, moths, beetles, and many other insects also do this important job.

They move from flower to flower, drinking nectar and spreading pollen.

honeybee

apple blossom

butterfly

lantana flower

In order for a lily to be pollinated, it needs pollen from another lily. Pollen from a rose or daisy won't help the lily flower make seeds.

# Hummingbird Pollinators

Insects aren't the only kind of animal that can pollinate flowers.

The tiny ruby-throated hummingbird visits flowers to lap up nectar with its long tongue.

While feeding, the bird hovers in the air by flapping its wings about 50 times in one second.

Pollen from the flower's anthers sticks to the bird's wings.

The bird then spreads the pollen to other flowers it visits.

**hibiscus flower**

Some plants don't need animal pollinators. Instead, they are pollinated by the wind. Their pollen is blown from one flower to another.

stigma

anthers

The flower in this picture is a hibiscus (hye-BIHS-kuhs). Try to describe the ways in which a hibiscus and a lily flower are the same and different.

ruby-throated hummingbird

# Bats Can Pollinate, Too!

Some types of bats visit flowers to eat pollen and drink nectar.

These small animals pick up pollen on their fur, and spread it as they fly from flower to flower.

The bats visit plants that produce fruits such as mangoes, figs, and peaches.

After the bats pollinate the flowers, the plants grow their seeds inside fruits.

In New Zealand, a type of lizard called a gecko climbs trees called pohutukawas (puh-hoo-tuh-KAH-wuhs) to drink nectar and eat pollen from the trees' fluffy, red flowers. The gecko carries the pollen from flower to flower on its skin.

gecko

pohutukawa flower

a bat feeding on
nectar at night

flower

19

# It's Teamwork!

When bees or other pollinators visit flowers, two very important things happen.

First, the animals get the food they need from the flowers.

Second, the flowers are pollinated by the animals and can make seeds.

When honeybees and lilies come together, they make a great team!

Bees pollinate apple blossoms. Then the blossoms make seeds, which grow inside the apples that people like to eat. Without bees, there would be no seeds and no apples!

# Pollination in Action

**1.** In the summer, a lily plant grows flowers. A bee visits the lily flower to drink its nectar.

**2.** Pollen from the lily's anthers sticks to the bee.

**3.** The bee flies to another lily. Some pollen on the bee's body sticks to this flower's stigma.

**4.** The flower uses pollen carried by the bee to make seeds. The seeds drop to the ground in the fall.

**5.** The seeds grow into new lily plants in the spring.

# Science Lab

Watch bees and other pollinators in action by growing some cosmos flowers for them to visit.

Here are some things to do when your flowers are fully grown:

- Look for pollen in their yellow centers.

- Keep a diary of the insects you see visiting the flowers.

- Watch for seeds forming in the centers of the flowers.

- Collect the seeds in an envelope.

- Next spring, plant the seeds and grow more cosmos flowers!

pollen

cosmos flower

cosmos flower seeds

## How to grow your cosmos plants

**Ask a grown-up to help you buy seeds online or from a garden center.**

❶ Packages of seeds have directions telling you when and how to plant them. You can plant your seeds in old yogurt cartons or flowerpots filled with potting soil.

❷ Place the containers in a sunny window.

❸ Water the seeds to keep the soil moist.

❹ Soon tiny seedlings will appear.

❺ When your plants are about three inches (7.6 cm) tall, plant them in a garden or in a larger flowerpot.

❻ If the soil gets dry, water your plants. In summer, your flowers will be ready for bees and other insects to pollinate them.

# Science Words

**anthers** (AN-thurz) the part of a flower that makes pollen

**hive** (HIVE) a honeybee's home where it lives with thousands of other bees

**pollen** (POL-uhn) a colorful dust made by flowers; flowers use pollen to help them make seeds

**pollination** (*pol*-uh-NAY-shuhn) the spreading of pollen from the anthers of a flower to the stigma, or stigmas, of a flower

**pollinators** (*pol*-uh-NAY-turs) animals that spread pollen from flower to flower so that the flowers can make seeds

**stigma** (STIG-muh) the part of a flower that receives pollen during pollination

23

# Index

# Read More

**Kalman, Bobbie.** *What Is Pollination? (Big Science Ideas).* New York: Crabtree (2011).

**Lundgren, Julie K.** *Seeds, Bees, and Pollen (My Science Library).* Vero Beach, FL: Rourke (2012).

**Slade, Suzanne.** *What If There Were No Bees? A Book About the Grassland Ecosystem.* Mankato, MN: Capstone (2011).

# Learn More Online

To learn more about pollination, visit
**www.bearportpublishing.com/Plant-ology**

# About the Author

Ellen Lawrence lives in the United Kingdom. Her favorite books to write are those about nature and animals. In fact, the first book Ellen bought for herself, when she was six years old, was the story of a gorilla named Patty Cake that was born in New York's Central Park Zoo.